A 3-minute forever book

EAT YOUR PEAS®

for an
Extraordinary
Young Person

By Cheryl Karpen
Gently Spoken

Dedicated
to
Maddy

to _____

from _____

At the heart
of this little book
is a
promise.

It's a promise from
me to you
and it goes like this...

If you ever need someone to talk to
(cry or brag with),
someone to hear
(really hear),
what's on your mind and in your heart,

Call me.

Call me early.   Call me late.   Just call me!

I promise to listen to you
with all my heart, with all my attention,
and without interrupting.

What's more,
I promise
to **cherish** you,
to lift you up
and (if I can help it)
never, ever let you down.

_____

My name

(Just in case you forgot who cares about you!)

_____

My phone #

Meanwhile,
here is my absolutely
no-strings attached
free advice
for getting the most out of
your amazing life.
Here goes!

You are enough.

You are
pretty or handsome
enough.

You are smart enough.

You are worthy enough.

You are enough just the way you are!

If only you could
see yourself through my eyes.

I see an amazing,
extraordinary,
bright, talented,
remarkable
YOU!

Comparing yourself
to others
will only make you unhappy.

Besides, it's a lot more fun
discovering
your own gifts
than copying someone else's.

Remember
to always be
kind and gentle
with
yourself.

Anything is possible.

Think twice
before deciding otherwise.

Life is filled with choices.

Choose carefully.

Always reach for,
wait for,
work for,
what will make you
feel alive
and
complete in life.

When you feel discouraged
or when life doesn't go
as you hoped it would—
believe.

There is a plan for you.

It's filled with
wonderful surprises
and it's greater than you ever imagined.

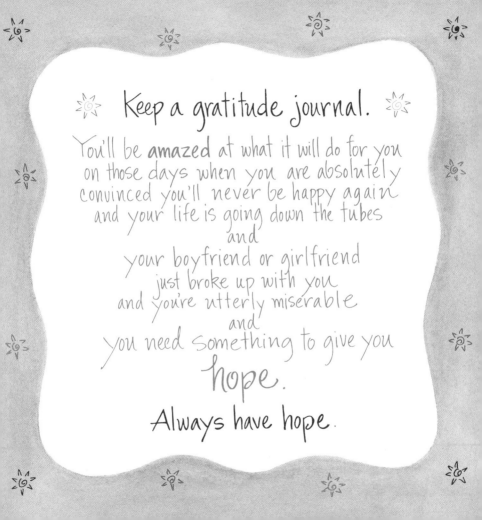

Keep a gratitude journal.

You'll be **amazed** at what it will do for you
on those days when you are absolutely
convinced you'll never be happy again
and your life is going down the tubes
and
your boyfriend or girlfriend
just broke up with you
and you're utterly miserable
and
you need something to give you
hope.

Always have hope.

Talk to yourself like you would talk to your own best friend:

You're awesome!

You look great!

You can do it!

Before you jump
to conclusions about another
amazing
(temporarily annoying)
human being,
put yourself in their shoes.

It may not be a perfect fit,
but you'll never forget the feeling.

We all make mistakes in life.

No one is perfect.

Not even those who
love you most.

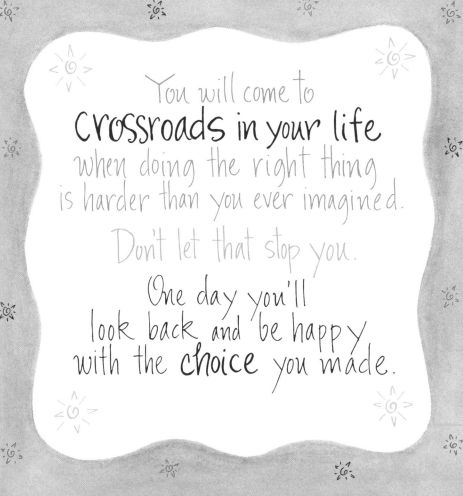

Accept change.
It's full of surprises you won't want to miss.

You can make
excuses
or
you can go out
and
make
a
difference!

You are a very important
Somebody.

No matter **where you have** come from,
no matter what **experiences** you have had,
no matter how crazy or sane you think
your **family** is,
no matter how large or small the **house** you live in is...

You are a very important
Somebody
and
no one can take your **magnificence** away!

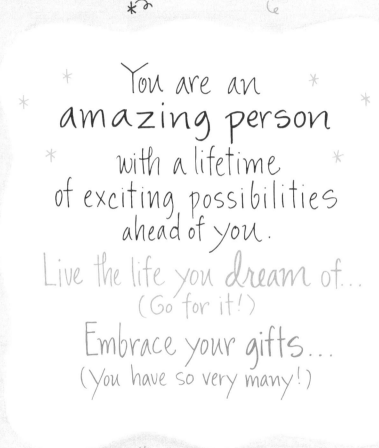

You are an
amazing person
with a lifetime
of exciting possibilities
ahead of you.
Live the life you dream of...
(Go for it!)
Embrace your gifts...
(You have so very many!)

Most of all,
stay healthy...
Eat Your Peas!

Why Peas?

She was a vibrant, dazzling young woman with a
promising future. Yet, at sixteen, her world felt sad and hopeless.

I was living over 1800 miles away and wanted to let this
very special young person in my life know I would be there for her
across the miles and through the darkness. I wanted her to know she could
call me anytime, at any hour, and I would be there for her. And I
wanted to give her a piece of my heart she could take with her
anywhere—a reminder she was loved. **Really loved.**

Her name is Maddy and she was the inspiration for my
first PEAS book, **Eat Your Peas for Young Adults.** At the very
beginning of her book I made a place to write in my phone number so she
knew I was serious about being available. And right beside the phone number
I put my promise to listen—*really listen*—whenever that call came.

Today Maddy is thriving and giving hope to others in her life.
If someone has given you this book, you must be a pretty amazing
person and they wanted to let you know it. Take it to heart.
Believe it, and remind yourself often.

Wishing you peas and plenty of joy,

Cheryl Karpen

P.S. My mama always said, "Eat your peas! They're good for you."
The tender and spirited words in this book are meant to be nutrition
for your heart and soul. Enjoy daily.

A portion of the profits from the
Eat Your Peas Collection
will benefit empowerment programs
for youth and adults.

If this book has touched your life,
we'd love to hear your story.
Please send it to
mystory@eatyourpeas.com
or mail it to
Gently Spoken
PO Box 245
Anoka, MN 55303

A very special
thank you to...
creative editor, **Suzanne Foust**
for her spirited play with words
and to
artist extraordinaire, **Sandy Fougner**
who ate, slept, and lived with
peas in her head
during the **creation** of this little book.

~ Cheryl

Three peas in a pod!

Suzanne Cheryl Sandy

About the author

"Eat Your Peas"

A self-proclaimed dreamer, Cheryl
spends her time imagining and creating
between the historic river town of Anoka, Minnesota
and the seaside village of Islamorada, Florida.

An effervescent speaker, Cheryl brings inspiration,
insight, and humor to corporations,
professional organizations and churches.
Learn more about her at: www.cherylkarpen.com

About the illustrator

Sandy Fougner artfully weaves
a love for design, illustration and
interiors with being a wife
and mother of three sons.

The Eat Your Peas Collection™

is now available in the following titles:

Daughters
Sons
Mothers
Sisters
Grandkids
Daughter-in-law

Girlfriends
Someone Special
Birthdays
New Moms
Tough Times
Extraordinary
   Young Person

New titles are SPROUTING up all the time!

Heart and Soul Collection

To Let You Know I Care
Hope for a Hurting Heart
Can We Try Again? Finding a way back to love

For more inspiration, Like us on Facebook at the Eat Your Peas Collection.
For quotes and pretties to post, follow us on Pinterest at
www.pinterest.com/eatyourpeasbook/

To view a complete collection of our products, visit us online at www.eatyourpeas.com

Eat Your Peas® for an Extraordinary Young Person

Homegrown in the USA

For more information or to locate a store near you, contact:
Gently Spoken
PO Box 245
Anoka, MN 55303

Toll-free 1-877-224-7886